The Time of the Night

Alex Katz b. 1927, *Place*, 1977, Oil on canvas, Overall: 108 x 144 in. (274.3 x 365.8 cm). Whitney Museum of American Art, New York; purchase, with funds from Frances and Sydney Lewis 78.23. Alex Katz/Licensed by VAGA, New York, NY. Photographed by Bill Jacobson

FLYING OBJECT

X O X

The
T I M E

of the
N I G H T

BY

Gerrit Henry

Edited by Marc Cohen

Foreword by John Ashbery

THE GROUNDWATER PRESS
Hudson, New York · 2011

Book Design by Brian Brunius.

Cover Image: Detail from the Frontispiece. Alex Katz b. 1927, *Place*, 1977, Oil on canvas, Overall: 108 x 144 in. (274.3 x 365.8 cm). Whitney Museum of American Art, New York; purchase, with funds from Frances and Sydney Lewis 78.23. Alex Katz/Licensed by VAGA, New York, NY. Photographed by Bill Jacobson

ISBN 978-1-877593-10-9
Library of Congress Control Number: 2010921352

ACKNOWLEDGMENTS

Some of these poems first appeared in the chapbook *Couplets and Ballades* (New York: Dolphin Press, 1998), the anthology *Blood & Tears: Poems for Matthew Shepard* (New York: Painted Leaf Press, 1999), and *American Poetry Review.*

John Ashbery's Foreword first appeared as the Introduction to Gerrit Henry's *The Mirrored Clubs of Hell* (New York: Arcade–Little, Brown, 1991). Reprinted in John Ashbery, *Selected Prose,* edited by Eugene Richie (Ann Arbor: University of Michigan Press, 2004; Manchester: Carcanet Press, 2004).

David Lehman's Appendix first appeared as the Introduction to Gerrit Henry's *The Lecturer's Aria* (New York: The Groundwater Press, 1989).

TABLE OF CONTENTS

The Time of the Night

FOREWORD
by John Ashbery

Gerrit Henry's poems are by turns, sometimes even simul-
taneously, bitter and very funny, wry and ecstatic, harrowing
and soothing. His subjects are pain and alienation, TV and the
movies, relationships with friends, lovers, and parents; life in
New York City and the price its transitory pleasures exact;
cruising in Village bars and celebrating one's birthday in a
psychiatric ward; God and death and AIDS. At times it seems
that he is about to tell us more about himself than he should
("I've gotten fat to discourage AIDS"), but he has the knack of
stopping just before he does so. (His stops are incredible and
heart-wrenching.) But in fact he isn't telling us about himself
to make us feel bad, or good, as some confessional poets have
done; he's not telling us about himself, not even telling.
Witnessing might be a better word, except that it sounds pre-
tentious and constrained. Instead his rhymes and rhythms are
those of the ballads of two poets he particularly admires: Cole
Porter and Lorenz Hart, yet always slightly off balance. The
metrical shoe never falls precisely at the place where we had
anticipated it would. This is but one of many strategies toward
an openness amounting to suspense, an unresolved chord at
the end. And the subjects listed above aren't precisely subjects,
but loci that stake out the territory he travels through, a Dante
adrift without a Virgil in the mirrored clubs of hell and their
surrounding cityscape: a world he never made but has accli-
mated himself to for the time being. No, the subject of his
poetry is poetry itself, in the broadest sense of the word: a voice
that moves toward and away from us and finally just stops, leav-
ing us with the feeling that we have just sensed life, though we
would be hard put to analyze it—and why not? Life is like that.

Perhaps the quintessential Henry poem is "The Watchers," in which the poet is writing the poem and at the same time watching on TV a horror movie so bad that even he considers abandoning it ("I am / Shocked and outraged / By the sheer ugliness / Of it all . . ."). But . . . "Will I turn it / Off? Probably, no. / I am lonely. And, in some // Subtle, subterranean way, / The movie gives me courage, / Just by its viciousness." But he doesn't stop there: at the end he is turning back to the typewriter to "write you, and me, / An alternative, / Write away the horror, / Write away the blood, / The inevitable, quick progression / Of another American night." In talking about writing an "alternative," Henry actually does so. The horror—and humor—of being trapped with a horror movie that can't even manage to be horrifying is quietly subsumed into "another American night" as the voice stops and the film continues to glimmer for a few seconds, like the point of light at the center of a television screen after you turn it off. Celluloid blood and gore, the poet's unrequited love affair with pop culture and his brief apostrophe to an unnamed "you," the traditional trappings of poetry and narrative which Henry is happy to avail himself of when they can further the work—all dissolve in a closure like that of a Brucknerian or Mahlerian adagio, a moment as transparent as a bubble that is about to burst. This is the splendor of his poetry, which is of a kind we haven't seen before.

PREFACE
by Marc Cohen

It seems like only yesterday and at the same time like decades ago that I received a call from the painter John Wells, Gerrit Henry's close friend and confidant, informing me that Gerrit had been found dead, the victim of a heart attack, in the single-room occupancy building where he had been living since 1995. The date of that call was May 1, 2003, the day President George W. Bush declared that we had reached the end of major combat operations in the Iraq war while standing in front of a large "Mission Accomplished" banner. The irony of having to share the stage with Mr. Bush on his last day on Earth would not have been lost on Henry, not because the Commander-in-Chief's statement turned out to be absolutely wrong, but because Henry was a strict grammarian who would not hesitate to correct anyone, and who deplored the president's butchering of the English language.

Two months later, I went to Gerrit's room and retrieved as many of his poems and other literary effects, including a novel, as I could find there, and I brought them back to my house in Sag Harbor. My effort in that regard turned out to be a kind of rescue mission, similar to the one performed by Kenneth Koch decades before, when he went to Frank O'Hara's New York City apartment with a suitcase as soon as he had heard of his friend's death, and filled it with every poem he could find, before anyone else could get to them, particularly family members who might not care for the content of some of the unpublished work. I spent the rest of the summer going through a couple of hundred poems that Henry had left behind, and it will come as no surprise to those who knew him well that many of the sheets of paper that they were typed or written on still smelled strongly of tobacco. While I read the poems every day, an exercise as much about keeping the dialogue between us going as about unearthing new Henry gems, I found a Last Will and Testament that appointed my wife, the poet Susan Baran, and me as his literary executors. The poems in this volume are selected from those papers; few have been published before.

It is important to note a few things about Henry's literary pedigree that perhaps even some of those who considered themselves close to him might not be aware of. First and foremost is the fact that John Ashbery's fourth book of poetry, *The Double Dream of Spring,* is dedicated to him. Koch, with whom Henry studied at Columbia, and from whose example he developed an ego-driven voice for his poems that would eventually turn much darker in tone than anything his professor would have written, introduced him to Ashbery, who inspired him to create longer narrative poems and encouraged him to write art criticism. Secondly, the late Richard Seaver, the editor who edited and published Henry's *The Mirrored Clubs of Hell,* under his Arcade imprint at Little, Brown and Company in 1991, was also instrumental in publishing such "rabble-rousers" as Samuel Beckett, Henry Miller, William Burroughs, and the Marquis de Sade in the United States. In Henry's work, Seaver certainly saw a poet who on some level had the same ability to strike a raw nerve with his readers and to stir them up. One just has to read "Hamlet," "Caprice #9," "Manic," "Two Boys," "Toxic," "On the Ward," "In a Blackish Mood," or "Credo Diabolique" from this collection to see why Seaver felt this way. Ashbery wrote an introduction for *The Mirrored Clubs of Hell,* which is included as the Foreword of this book at the suggestion of Eugene Richie, the poet who edited Ashbery's *Selected Prose,* and who, along with his wife, the poet Rosanne Wasserman, founded and runs The Groundwater Press, which published Henry's chapbook *The Lecturer's Aria* in 1988 as part of the Intuflo Editions series.

Finally, as far as influences and mentors are concerned, the reader should be aware that the Jimmy in the poem "Jimmy Yawned" is James Schuyler, whom he met through Ashbery. Henry admired the concise and precise language Schuyler employed in his poetry and in conversation, and because both had spent time in psychiatric wards, he considered Schuyler a kind of kindred spirit as well.

A note on a few other poems: "The Confessions of Gerrit II," which appears in this volume, is preceded by "The Confessions of Gerrit I," included in *The Mirrored Clubs of Hell* and reprinted in 1988 as part of the Macmillan *Best American Poetry* anthology series. As far as I can tell, "Caprice #9" stands alone as a poem and is not part of a series.

I would like to thank John Ashbery, Susan Baran, Douglas Baxter, Thomas Breidenbach, Robert Harms, Alex Katz, David Lehman, Eugene Richie, Bill Sullivan, Rosanne Wasserman, and John Wells for their help with and their crucial support of this project.

The Time of the Night

To My Audience

To entertain, and to console:
These are my only goal,
And, surely, to make myself sigh,
And, maybe, to make your time fly.

But not to be particularly poetic—
It's more like some verbal athletic

I aspire to with my words,
Dumb as the chatter of birds.

So I ask you to stay awhile.
Don't make faces, or force a smile,

But take what you like, and leave the rest.
Maybe these reasons aren't the best,

Or the only ones, but they'll serve.
I grant you, it takes consummate nerve

To impose on you even this little bit
If what I consider to be pearls, you consider shit.

Just listen carefully, please,
Or I will never find peace.

To be consoled, to be entertained:
That is your hope, my only gain.

JACOB AND THE ANGEL

What is your goal in life?
"To get more sleep,
And be kinder to old ladies in front of me
On the street, whom I long to shove."

Have you ever raped anyone?
"Hardly."
Whom do you love?
"Only myself
A loved one told me."

To whom do you answer
When it comes down to it?

"My family.
I have no wife
Or particular landscape in mind."

How tired can you get
Before collapsing?

"I never collapse.
I call friends after an all-nighter,
And suck life from them
A little after dawn—the reverse of Dracula.
This they seem to mind."

What else do you see as your goal?
"To be a poet."
Again.
"To be a writer
Which I am."

4

Then why write poems?
"Out of self-sufficiency."
Did your mother satisfy you?
"The high point of my career.
I know one mother who didn't
Suffer postnatal depression,
Although her children did.
Is that enough of an answer?"

Why are you so unhappy?
"The rules of the game.
We all screw around.
I play, you play, no one acts."

Hmm. How are you at parties?
"I keep a stylish distance away from friends
And posit myself, existentially,
On a chair or any available lounger.
And I try to keep my trap shut.
I don't drink much anymore."

You don't drink at all?
"White wine spritzers—two of them.
I more worship at sweet marijuana's shrine
If and whenever possible
Then pass out on the family collie."

I thought you never collapsed?
"I don't. I pass out.
This is my main goal in life."

I thought your main goal was sleep?
"Everybody's doing it.

That's why I pass out.
I can do anything, after a little rest."

Do you consider yourself demon-possessed?
"Without precedent."
And God?
"Occasionally He helps
Me find lost things."

That's St. Anthony.
"Oh . . . well, God's a good fellow, too.
I guess. Absolutely marvelous.
Although I could do without
The overemphasis on the little matter of sex."

Do you like sex?
"I used to, before
I became a nun of sorts."

A nun?
"Oh, all right,
A prioress."
We're almost through now.
I sense the dawn.

"Oh great! I mean, oh, gee."
You haven't enjoyed this?
"Does a lamb enjoy his shearing,
A woman her last breath?"

That's it. Time.
"Oh, gee.
Can I ask you a question?"

No.
"I've wrestled from midnight
Until daybreak,
And you won't give me a name?
I've lost my real one
Through this."

Yes. No. Yes.
I name you Adele Astaire.

"Adele Astaire?"
Drop it. One final question.
Do you realize there are people around who like you,
Who are concerned for your welfare,
And that you're letting them down a little bit more each day?

"This shoe is purely on the other foot.
I'll give it some thought before I dream,

If I dream, as if I knew, or could.
People who like me? Who care?
No one cares as much as I do, Angel.
There isn't enough sand in the sea
Or time in the air. Adele Astaire?"

BIG THEMES

Virtue is other people's
definition of love. Fate
has no propriety.

Life is a substratum
of big themes. Tanglewood
is Tanglewood, geographically, musically.

Grace is no instant arbiter of form
nor is youth always that captivating,
nor does the key exactly fit in the dorm.

Soul is a waste of time,
without death. Without
waste, life is a time of soul.

ROMANZE

for John Ashbery

Tod and his companion
Stood stock-still with their lanterns,

Awestruck at what could not be:
The fresh-dug tomb was empty!

But hadn't Rosalinde just been laid
In that dark stinking grave,

And hadn't shovelfuls of stone
Hit the coffin with a hollow groan?

Tod's companion fell back against a tree,
Gasping for breath, and to be set free

From this vision of very likely horror
He would have to avow, on his honor,

While his chum, a choking Tod
Offered himself up to God,

For where Rosalinde had been by man laid to rest,
Nature knew better, and now God the best.

AUGUST

Under the catalpa tree, fanning itself
like a jaded peacock, you tell me
a story you have told before:
it concerns an old man in Tuscany who said
he valued love more than his riches.
He gave away his riches to his lover boy
who invested in him, doubled them
and left with the money in a boat
with a yellow sail. The sail was so
yellow you say that it blazed like the sun;
like the sun, I repeat, snapping
off grass blades and arranging them
in a circle on my lap. And the old man, you say,
was left to wander distractedly and beg
in the streets. The old man's name was
Alonzo known ever after as The Great Lover
and the boy lover's name was Giorgio
known ever after as The Crafty One and
he married a mulatto dancer in Madrid
and I look up at the catalpa tree
which drops a leaf courteously in my lap
in my circle of grass blades and I say
Come to the point: tell me
you're leaving me.

AUGUST II

I don't want to let
This day pass without marking it—
August sun royale, a dry breeze,
Without clouds sparking it—

This feeling you have
Of Scottish summer finally passing—
The new look, the gilded light, the liberty
Of the people on the street, massing

With each other, gladly,
For once, as they walk.
This is not sentimentality,
Summer cabin fever, or mere talk

We're finding here, but
Autumn, warming the climatic bench
At last, here quite soon, with its
Longer nights, dead leaves, and cleaner stench.

August Idyll

Sometimes I leave my Cross pen
On my desk, as if there will
Be something to do.
I don't take you everywhere
Anymore, since you went away.

You were a fool, but I bless
Your thriving heart. Now
I'm alone, still dreaming
Of the Azores. And I can't stand it:
Can't stand the dense, impenetrable heat
Nor the secret torturers of August,
And I can't stand there
Being no writing to do, boo-hoo.

I'm poor, but not by design,
Lazy, but not by choice.
My life, God, is ever
More persistent folly. Oh
That the crow would sing ceremoniously,
And love be heard.
I'm lonely out of necessity.

ODE TO A FRIENDSHIP

Can you understand
What kind of proof
Of ownership must
Go into this simple
Sign? What fetid bait;
What frippery and tired
Frolic; what wholesome
Malaise; infinity of
Report; vapid rumor
Of immortalizing accident
Or injury; what penurious,
Yet innocent design?

I owe you all I have, so's
I must keep mine. Strange,
How the mountain slopes upward
Here and there, even
On a downward climb. Strange,

How we met, saw, developed
Things. Strange, for
Our otherwise troubled times.

TEN MINUTES

I have ten minutes to get happy,
Before I meet John Penn at the infamous Argo.
Quick, a jester! Some unsubtle irony
Or something. Paging Bette Midler!

My mood has just brightened
Considerably since I realized I was
Having dinner with somebody I like a lot,
And whose poetry I "admire," as Kenneth used to say
When jealous of his position, or overpoweringly met.
But it's not enough. I may depress him—

Except I sense strange things are happening
Neither he nor I want to miss,
The Second Coming, with neither Christ nor anti-Christ
Involved, quite beside the point as they've become
Something's coming . . . I'm leaving . . .
Happy now I've realized this best and worst
Of times in the allotted ten minutes, just ten minutes.

RICHARD

Richard seldom complained,
Although he'd refer to it a lot in jokes.
I stood continually in the shadow
Of my own, ongoing awe at it, and fear for,
His grinning perseverance,
Richard's righteous refusal to abandon
A native strength, an interior solidity—
"Force of soul," as Henry James described it—
Crossed with a humble, unfeigned docility
That everyone else took as a patient waiting-for-the-end.

Richard. I would go over to his place
On Saturday nights, almost every one
For those two years' time of a sentence
They couldn't yet commute, for pizza or Japanese,
Fave videos, and joints. He'd roll one fat one for himself,
And one fatter one for me, because of his AIDS.
He was like that, thoughtful; although I could tell
It chagrined him, hurt his pride, that we couldn't share one.
Basically, though, he didn't give a damn.
He was also like that. His disease didn't offend him,
Or me, I know now, nor did less and less affect us
As the two-year interval rolled by.

Three times he was in Doctors Hospital with pneumonia.
"Why Doctors Hospital, Richard?" I'd demand to know,
"With banana heiress across the hall
Recovering from plastic microsurgery
And the woman who had her baby in a mink in a cab?"
He didn't know. His doctor wouldn't explain.
Some of the nurses would wear gauze masks
Over their mouth and nose, the elastic disappearing

Gamely into their pertly coiffed hair, this well after science
Had disproved any risk of contagion from the air.
Sometimes, they would slide his breakfast tray
From the hallway with their foot, into his room,
And dash off to another impatient facelift patient.
Richard did complain once—
Or rather staged some excellent,
Hospital-ward psychodrama by throwing his dinner tray
At a grudging attendant clear cross the room,
All the way from his elevated bed.
Secretly thrilled, I castigated him for this:
"You've got to get along with them, Rich, please?"
Richard, I've almost given up the pot,
Like you wanted me to do, and you wanted to as well.
Though we just couldn't. I had no excuse but boredom.
But could Jahweh Himself blame you
In your glaze-eyed gratitude for this relieving vice?
Richard, maybe you're with Jahweh right now,
Or Zeus, or Allah, or the Christ who rules
Those other angels from the Church of the Ascension,
Where you had been proudly taken in, a token of the times.
It was almost as if you congratulated yourself
For your want of needing anyone; at the same time,
You seemed unavoidably eager to leave for parts indistinct,
Not yet ready to be known. Two years ago today
You died in a rail-guard bed in Intensive Care,
With the heart-crisis patients, ironically.
When I got there—and, Lord knows, I had delayed my coming—
I was amazed. I was afraid of you and your heaving torment,
You were so viciously and willfully gasping for air,
Like, God forgive me, a beached blowfish,
Opening your wide brown eyes briefly
To stare mournfully and fearfully into mine,
As if in reproach, I felt, although terror was more like it,

When I took your hand, as the nurse encouraged me to do.
"Talk to him," she said, half-admonishingly.
There are all kinds of heroes. I didn't know what to say.

Richard, I want you to now know I know
The truth you knew, had been gifted with
And never kept from me, even when it hurt to talk.
In our rambling, elliptical, increasingly Kierkegaardian
Conversations over the last few months, we'd talked about it,
Although neither could put his finger on it, exactly. Who can?
You are the absence in my daily life I phone friends for.
Richard, there's no word for it but terrible.
And Richard, you should have complained.

HAMLET

Death is a transient location:
The steep of a godforsaken mountain, a spindly forest,
Not a virtual lifetime vocation,
Wailed in ecstatic male chorus.

I'm so . . . thrilled to be here!
Which dagger should I plunge in first,
And where, in which inviolate organ?
Shall I read from Fanny Chatterley or Fannie Hurst?

My sister—had I had one—would I have loved,
But not so much as her brother, too.
Does this alarm you? I say it from love
Corporeally withheld from too many by too many of you.

S'pose you jes' hides behin' this curtain,
Until God decides if Gertrude would be nice
Or if "no one gets out of here alive!"—
Take the chance, be the lad, do the vice.

I frighten myself less and less these days,
Which even I find frightening.
It's more a curse when they've come to stay.
In renouncing you, my joy has been like lightning.

It's more of a curse when they've come for no good.
Shall I remain 1) alone 2) aloof 3) appearing bitter,
When I also enjoy gossiping with my mother
And when I, the irascible runt, am the pick of the litter?

I find it striking how it might astound you
Just before you go limp and explode.

Until God decides if Gertrude will serve,
I'll trade my bad habit for a toad.

For a habit has got me: the habit of habit,
Which leaves little time for or recourse to anything else.
You curse me for it? Then I'll cure you first.
I'll pet your ass. I'll smooth back your pelt.

Oh Lord that in life Death were more demonstrable!
Who could hate himself more, with such wings of stone?
And why not that men with men aren't welcomed fairly?
My only sin is to insist I sin alone.

SEVEN POEMS IN ONE

Two Poems, Same Day

1. Two-Part Invention

    Because I've been forsaken,
    I heretofore forsake my God.
    His nights, anyway, are a holy terror;
    My vast troubles with Him bore

    Even me. Oh, pray, enemy-cum-friend,
    Pray for me. There has been
    Some kind of massive error
    From the start, which has left me
    So inappropriate to this life,
    I don't dare pray for myself anymore.
    And I have myself no prayerful wife.

2. Three Child Stars

    I've been at so many
    Beginnings-of-the-end,
    Even more at ends-of-the-beginning,
    That my head is on backwards for good,
    The twisted-180-degrees-stationary look
    We all know so well, courtesy of
    William Peter Blatty, and his crony, Linda Blair.
    Remember the days when that little shocked?

    "Oh, I'll be nice from
    Now on, Auntie Em.
    I went to Hell, and now I rue it!

"I won't bother the chickens
Anymore, I promise, or balance
Myself on the hog pen." Poor
Dorothy. She went home again,
Which none can do, even forsaking
Oz. Simply put, she blew it.

Third of a Sequence, That Same Night

Has it ever occurred
To you that America's
Obsession with violence
Is not purely American,
Unlike everything else we do?

"It all comes out
In the wash, anyway." Well,
Yes—but people have died
Or gone crazy from it!

"Tough shit!
That's the wash
I was talking about!"

Good Lord—get out!!
But you, my fancied friend,
You—struggle to stay alive
And find out the truth,
Even if it kills you,
All those little Hells.

Nothing can harm you if you do.
Sinners, look to yourselves!

Sequence Finale, Before Soup Dinner

My poetry, which you've
Seen here, is all I have.
I hope it gives you cheer.
It's what I do,
Like extensive gardening,
Or collecting trash.

Therefore, Mother, a bit more bargaining.
Sis, don't turn to wasting ash!
But, try to take my poetry away—
Trust me—by Zeus, you will die!
But not yet I, dear counselors,
Not I!

Postlude, Before Reading to Audrey

I'm sorry that you couldn't take
This particular one of the many calls I make
To you, night and day.
It seems you had no other way

To handle self, mother, and child
Without being driven absolutely wild.
So I'm writing this as I wait for your call.
Really, I don't mind at all.

To be honest, I was thinking of marrying you, before,

But you haven't divorced yet, and what's more,
I have no way at all with women—
At least, mother and sister. I hope you're a given.

So don't neglect to call me soon,
Or I may fall off into an awful swoon
Upon which could float no rescue ship, fore or aft.
I would expire alone with my lone and sullen craft.

Prequel: Marc and Susan and Larry Sanders

I don't do well under discipline.
People can't do their work
When they're shitting in their pants.

"My place is clean.
You wanme to clean your place?"
Oh, God, time to face
The void again,
Unalloyed again.

It gets better; believe me:
Funnier, suaver than Cary Grant.
He should have, but he can't.
"I'm sorry you had to know."
Sorry, I've gotta do the show.

Sequel: for Ann-Margret as "Blanche"

Yes, I know.
It's too late.
I already know.
And here I stand.

Which one was the blow
That settled my fate?
I already know,
Familiar signposts of land

Ahoy! If you can go that far,
Who is going to continue to star?
If you can still believe,
Well, I can just leave—

Well, no, no, not yet.
Things are so much brighter,
And these common ones are the best I get;
It doesn't get any lighter,
And I dangle there, a paranoid marionette.

NEAR THE OCEAN

for James Henry

I remember another October just like this—
It was last year.
The air was as fragrant as a boy's kiss,
And the sky twice as clear.

Election Day fell in there somewhere, too,
And June-warm Halloween night.
We'd waited all fall for word of you.
By early November, the word was blight.

Parties continued, and writing for pay,
In the chilly October air.
I remember, I taught some classes at S.V.A.
While I prattled on, you lingered there.

The lingering became a kind of last profession,
As autumn months inevitably succeeded,
A kind of proof of ownership, and earthly secession—
That you still desperately needed.

Now it's plucky and pliable October again
And soon it will be February,
The month of your death—but who remembers when?
The cemetery was soaked in sun, and airy,

But I'm getting ahead of the story.
Soon, Thanksgiving was called off,
And I started working on the complete picture of your glory.
Early December, early January, late January, I hauled off

And went up there, but by then you only lay and smiled like a
    puppet.
Actually, come to think of it, it is now November.
By last December, I knew nothing could stop it,
Like a song or legend you suddenly remember.

RELIGION

Religion? I don't
Know. Things just seem
To go along on their
Own, well or unwell.
Often well, knock wood,
Because you're usually
Lucky, knock wood. (There

Is some dispute about
Whether, in knocking
Wood, you are not knocking for
The protection of tree
Spirits, or the wood of
The cross.) Which just

Proves my argument: by
His very nature, God
Must love us all, Christian,
Non-Christian or
Un-Christian, if He is
To be God. I'm not sure,

Though, that that's
The point. It's just that

Today I'm content. And
If Christ sits on God's
Right hand, who's
At His left?

The Time of the Night

1.
This is the time of the night
When the sun, setting, sings
And lovers grow gauzy wings

This is the time of the night
When we raise an oblivious shout
To help the moon come out

It's the time of the night
When the lordly hawk
Must give up his lonely stalk

The exact time of the night
When fervent anticipation
Begets flagrant self-degradation

This is the time of night
For a genuine sense of fright
At the thought of not getting tight

The sense of the best to come
A sense that some rest will come

It's that time of night
When, if snow is felt
It's already begun to melt.

2.
Or, if rain intrudes
It's the smell of spring it exudes

Or, if witches fly
It's only to hasten by.

3.
This is the time of night
When death is wholly remembered
Considered, then casually tendered

Toward which the day has been heading
Old nightshirts and rumpled bedding

When boys out in their convertible
Cruise the streets, unhurtable

4.
It's the time of night
When the mind gets rather lazy
And thinking, easefully hazy

The time of night
When good sense calls it quits
And everything goes to bits

It's the very time of night
When life is more than it seems
And time will soon stop for dreams

APRICOT NECTAR

They can't be any more than
Hints, because we're not sure:
The real look of happy surprise
On the face of the man behind the mask;
A circular stripe of orange sunset
Beneath a star-choked blue sky above;
Certain Bach and Respighi, all Mozart;
The lack of any real pretense so far
In this person you would like to know better;
The pages of a family-Bible-sized dictionary
Lovingly riffled by a searching summer breeze;
Long, impassable winters; an indescribable face.
Oh, we can't be sure of anything
But native citizenship and certain old memories.
Still, I'll stand behind the notion
At hand, that we live to further ends,
That the truth be spoken and love be heard,
Too discreetly wonderful to be anything
More than half-hidden from us now,
Too simple for us to ever elaborate on, even then.

THE POSTULANT

for Marc Cohen

I love you,
but I love you
in a very selfish way.
There must be some other
design for living.

Will I go?
Should I sit up at last?
Shall I stay?
What is charity,
and what is the price of giving?

Few men have been
as lucky as I,
few men as gifted from without,
fewer nearly touching the sky,
still fewer knowing what it may all be about.

I love you,
but I love you
as if you were me.
What more could I ask for?
Who else could I hope to be?

CAPRICE #9

The Panadol in the blue box
Need not be in the briefcase,
Just as the Prokofiev concerto
Could be turned off.
He had lovely hair, but it burned off
When the comets hurtled through space.

I like it, though, a little,
With lilacs stinking up the room.
You turn on the tap-faucet,
Rather, and slurp water.
He changed his mind about the king's daughter,
Ever after radiating an aura of gloom.

The story could correctly
Be read as mystery or romance,
Where you spend all your time
Working in solitary confinement.
If I could just remember how that line went,
We could get up and dance.

Enviably paupered and frail,
He was the only one to give it a shot.
We played doubles for nothing,

And you all the time huffing and puffing.
But to me it meant an awful lot.

RECESSION

I suffer much from even handling
The natty little copper 'n' black
Sony Walkman I bought on a monstrous spree
Late last summer—"I want the top-
Of-the-line Sony," I said to the puzzled
Salesman, not so puzzled that
He couldn't produce it—perhaps he thought
I was merely looking for a "best buy."
I think I bought the two twin black-
Plastic Sony Mini-Speakers that
Day, too. They sound so good
Together; I suffer much, as well,
From using them, together,

Mainly because it's near December
And I've paid AmEx only a small,
If sizeable, fraction of last summer's
Magnificently ill-timed, personal stimulating-of-
The-economy, and I sense, or can figure,
That I haven't yet covered copper 'n' black
Walkman or black-plastic speakers.
I might venture a guess they'll be
Taken care of on some far-off day,
Well beyond winter, in a hard-won
Monthly installment. But I suffer most

From freely enjoying Mega-Bass squawkboxes
And 9-Preset-Radio-Station Auto-Reverse—
They aren't mine, and they're no one else's.
Yet the sound they make is Steinway,
As far as personal stereos go,
The digital tracking incorrigible,

The handiness on desk or night table heavenly.
So I play Judy's "Alone," John McGlinn's
First-time incomplete "Annie Get Your Gun"
(With coyly Mermanesque Annie), Nielsen's
Symphonies One and Six, Judy's "Alone,"
Mahler's maddened orchestration of the Schubert
Quartet, "Death and the Maiden," John
McGlinn's "Annie," Schumann quartets
(Never the lieder, if I can help it),
A certain Brahms sonata (he was corpulent,
You know, and smoked vile cigars) and Randy
Travis, whom to see in person
Would be sure bloodletting of the heart.
And tonight, on a very minor binge

At Tower Records—cash, mind you—
I bought a "Requiem" and "Magnificat"
By Orlando Lassus, having fallen unrequitedly
In love with the "Lamentations of Jeremiah,"
And am playing it now, at 3 A.M.-ish,
And the mini-monolith speakers
And the cock-of-the-walk Walkman are
Paid for in Heaven,
At least in the coin of the realm.

MRS. HENRY

In some odd way, she understands
Exactly what I go through.
It's not intuitive.
It's more a matter of life.

She is all things,
And everything else, too.
It's not a case of instinct,
Or even the habit of a wife—

She's just there.
And when I turn away,
It's awful, the lunar
Landscape that I see.

She is the rain, the river,
The questing smile,
All substance,
And all mystery.

SUMMER, THURSDAY EVE

Lying on the couch,
As always, I meant to pick
Up *The Christian Science
Journal* with its blissful
Metaphysics, but wound up
Somehow settling back
With the *National Enquirer,*
Instead. "Uh, boy," I
Thought, but was soon
Raptly reading the latest
Astonishing episode of "The
Delta Burke Story," in which
She battles mental illness—
And wins! said the cover.
It was much sleazier a story
Than that; my eyes kept being
Diverted to the photos, as I
Scrutinized them for the manner
In which she made herself look
Less fat—but the porcine
Face kept giving it all away,
For all the knee-length
Pink spangle-sweaters and out-
Of-the-bottle—a Duane Reade
Bottle, from the motley
Look of it—bleach job. I
Read on, thoroughly
Perusing the *Enquirer,*
To an article about "Laughter
Therapy," which I liked—
The idea, I mean. I'd heard
About it before, in Uris 8

At Lenox Hill, but I
Wasn't in the best of moods
For trying it then,
So I tried it again,
Thinking of a close friend's
Recent on-target joke about himself,
Laughed, and felt better.
Yet on the second-to-
Last page, a story about
Dwarf couples adopting dwarf
Children as a hobby disgusted
Me with myself. I let the *Enquirer*
Fly to the floor, next to
The half-open *Christian Science*
Journal—"No! That," I thought,
"Was bizarre enough!" The *Journal*'s
Still there for another time, al-
Though now the night stretches
Out before me like all of Mongolia.
July—it's the dead
Of the year, for the living.

How Quickly

How quickly things
Turn into their opposites:
Lust, a lonely desire,
Self-pity, a sainthood,
Hope, pure affection.
Will we make it through
Again to the improbable
Beginning? Is there a need to?
What color stands for passage,
And is it indeterminate, its wish
For love's unfathomable bias?

As long as it sounds
Like there's some argument
Going on, however mutely.
As long as the longing ego
Is put to bed, and bedded.
Encouragement comes only
At night, from the stars.

That way, Halloween and Patriots' Day
Are in your honor, too.
It takes so much mindless doing,
This seeking to be at ease.

So we must generate this very ending
That hastens, like yesterday, to overtake us,
Like fine, feckless reason
And reasoning's scattered constituency,
The saint learning all about it
As he quickly fills his plate,
The grosser portion
Of love confounded.

SISTERS

To grief, you've added grief,
To tears, unendurable sobs.
Denying me either calm or relief
Has become both your jobs.

"Her" cuts me off from "she,"
While "she" makes excuses for "her."
It's like some Jacobean tragedy,
Where the trees are all astir.

I tell you what we'll do:
I'll drop out of sight,
Which will make at least one of you happy,
The gold of your delight.

My sign will become the Moon,
Wishful, transitory, bright,
If only relative to the day,
And finished every night.

MANIC

Play the most terrible music!
Stay the awful clowns!
This simply isn't funny,
These intractable ups and downs,

Being constantly on the lam
From a horseman known as Night.
It is, finally, as I please:
The bounty uncovers the blight,
The staying-up until Doomsday,
And staying alive past dawn,
Knowing the earth is on fire,
And the animals on the lawn.

The comfort of the intellect
Turn to sawdust and spume,
And I've never wanted to live so much,
And I've never so dreaded this room!

My Affairs

My affair with Andy Warhol
Lasted fifteen minutes.
My affair with Deborah Kerr
Was an affair not to remember.
During my affair with Liz, or Elizabeth,
I put on seventy pounds.
An ensuing affair with Richard Simmons
Took care of a lot of that.

My affair with Claire Trevor
Was a whispered affair,
Effortlessly witty and perfumed with poison.
My affair with Pierre Trudeau
Left me with a deep dislike for stretch limos.
My affair with Thomas Mann
Faltered a milligram up the Magic Mountain.
I drank a lot of coffee to sit up nights with him,
In my affair with poor Marcel Proust, moonchild deluxe.
During my affair with Joan Rivers
I put my fingers in my ears and sang
Loudly every time she opened her mouth.
My affair with Mick Jagger
Still doesn't surprise me, nor did it him.

My affair with Barbara Bush was
Bothersome due to her "scented" deodorant.
My affair with Roger Grimsby made the news.

Melanie Griffith was sexy, but she was
Always ending our affair in the papers.
My affair with President Clinton
I'm breaking to *The Chelsea Clinton Observer.*

My affair with Frederic Chopin—the child—
Ruined poor old George Sand,

Though she hadn't far to go.
My affair with Alfred Hitchcock
Consisted of a fat, black silhouette,
And a skinless Cornish hen.

During our affair, Gwen Verdon
Kept making persimmon-noses at me.
My affair with Helen Keller
Was the blind leading the blind.
My greatest affair, though,
Is with my audience,
For whom I'd gladly die—
Unless I could have an affair
With, say, the perky Tom Cruise?
Although my affair with Emilio
Estevez—well, things could have gone better.
He kept wanting a reason for having an affair.

Jamie Lee Curtis Has Gotten Me
through the Evening

Jamie Lee Curtis has gotten me through the evening.
Jamie Lee Curtis, silver-spoon offspring
Of Janet Leigh and Tony Curtis, who started slow
In *Halloween*—slow, but smart, scary—
Then just seemed to be hanging around the backlots
In a variety of ungratifying, undemanding roles
(Even *A Fish Called Wanda,* I fear) has finally hit
Her post-ingénue, comic stride in *True Lies,*
Matching Arnold Schwarzenegger tone for tone,
Nuance for nuance (yes, Arnold Schwarzenegger)
Milking nothing but what's there,
Reconciling glamour with jokes, attitude with truth,
Mugging little but revealing much—
About the absurdity of Hollywood action movies,
The lonely heroics of being born into Tinseltown royalty,
And most of all her fresh, cool self,
Her lack of pretension and off-the-beam beauty.
It is almost over; don't let it be over.
Let's all have another reel or two.
It is almost October; it is Sunday night,
That most dismal of weekly events
And I am nothing if not frightened,
Full of old teeth and tired disapproval,
Except of Jamie Lee Curtis,
Who got me through the evening
Leaving me with nothing feasible
To get me through the night.

GERRIT THE ACTOR

I do wild things with my eyes, still.
I used to do them with my whole face—
A small-time Broadway producer once told me,
When I was drunk, on a jet to L. A.,
"You should have been an actor!
You have a very expressive face."

Now, twenty hastening years later,
I have very expressive eyes.
The rest of my face more or less hangs,
Inexpressive, even sullen, immobile
As the eyes of a Buddhist saint.
I have carry-all bags under my lids,
And my bee-stung lips have come unstung,
But the eyes still have it, alone.
They're not blue, as
With all major movie stars;
Still, they're not brown, either,
As with many minor ones.
They're a tomcattish shade of hazel,
And they open wider than the similar eyes
Of children—or so I dream, so I hold,
In thought, and in my open heart.
Sometimes, they roll, when I
Intuit something I can't believe;
Other times, they reel,
When I'm amazed at it all; or, finally,
They fly, fly right out of my head,
Across the endless room,
When I see someone over there
I want to notice my eyes.

And sometimes, they are silent,
Silent as pitch, silent as still belief.
Harry Rigby, the producer, was right:
I should have been an actor,
Or could have been.
Now, only my eyes are dramatic,
As if I had a very big part

In my own, continuing life story,
As the fifteen-year-old kid
Who wanted to be an actor,
But whose parents wouldn't let him,
Who has learned to tell the story,
Exclusively with his eyes.

HOMOSEXUALS IN THE MOVIES

Homosexuals in the movies
Never go to church.
They go to lunch.

Homosexuals in the movies
Are never seen lying down.
If they stand up, it is to fall.
They have no last names at all.

Homosexuals in the movies
Often go to their own reward
Soon into the picture.
Rarely are they featured.
Their first names are indistinct.

They usually have a hard time of it.
Often, they are funny, if not hilarious.
Rarely are they hilarious,
In anybody's movies,
Especially those of homosexual directors,
Of which there are a few.
I will not bother to name them.
You know their work,
If you've chatted with your homosexual relatives.
Some of them are foreign—not your relatives.
Homosexual directors.

Their lives only become believable
After the disaster.
Their existence is unfeasible,
And never long, and never sweet.

But homosexuals in the movies,
If they aren't villains, are sweet.
You see, Hollywood is sweet on them,
So many have been stars.
But homosexual stars never play
Homosexual characters.
If they did, who would know the difference?

Homosexuals in the movies
Start to act funny
If they let it get to them.
They never have boyfriends—just companions.
They are as alone as a Christmas tree.

They don't always look like Rock Hudson.
Sometimes they look like Montgomery Clift,
Or like the late George Sanders,
And act that way, too.
What way? Homosexuals in the movies
Are often British. They can sound like Harvey Fierstein.
More's the pity, they can look like him, too,
Especially when played by Harvey Fierstein.
Now where did they find him?
Homosexuals in the movies have to do without—
As do viewers, still, at the millennium.
Maybe especially at the second millennium.

THE CONFESSIONS OF GERRIT II

I don't own a microwave oven,
Like everyone else I know and love.
I think Delta Burke is still a striking woman.
My favorite show is *The Sound of Music*,
Especially the song, "You Are Sixteen Going on Seventeen,"
And the queer, winsome little dance that follows.
I think Jeff Koons is the greatest American artist since Keith
    Haring.
I don't read too many of the magazines I write for—
Or many others, for that matter. I'm too easily distracted.
I'm a Walkman person. I'd love a private jet for that.
I believe in the old adage, "A pill for every ill,"
A highly unfashionable sentiment these days.
But, "Let's say no" to drug hysteria, huh?
Some of them can be very helpful to the neurasthenic.
George Bush reminds me of Frank Morgan
As "The Wizard of Oz," except Morgan seemed more
    intelligent.

In high school, I used to intentionally wear green on
    Thursday.
I'm forty-two, and I live in a three-story walk-up—
Emphasis here on the "walk" and the "up."
I fall in love with the people who hurt me the most deeply.
I figure, no one else knows me better.
For some reason, my weeks were darkened, some weeks ago,
By the news of the suicide of Hollywoodite Anton Furst,
The set designer for *Batman* and Valium addict.
At one point, it could have been me leaping from that garage
    roof.

For heaven's sake—it could have been Liza Minnelli!
In summing up, I'd like to announce that I'm now available
For weddings, simple "hits," and brisses.
The art world hasn't been doing well lately,
And although I think they asked for it,
I'm missing out on those old toney catalogue essays,
And I have a lovely Irish tenor.
I wish I knew what it was like not to feel afraid.

NIXON

Unlike my good poetic
Pal John Ashbery, I seldom get
A title before I write the poem,
If ever . . . Other times, they're easy.
Anyway, how did director Oliver
Stone make the film drocudama—
Excuse me, docudrama—*Nixon* without
Having it turn out a comedy?
Anthony Hopkins neither looks,
Sounds, nor acts like the real thing,
The Richard Milhaus Nixon we all
Knew and didn't love and came
To detest; and Madeline Kahn
As Martha Mitchell? A bit of wish
Fulfillment in that, as in "You
Wish!" I have caught this moment

At a glance, with nothing much else
To do. Now Stone is restaging, proto-virtual
Reality-style, the famed Kennedy-
Nixon debates, with Hopkins on one side
Of the desk, in black and white, and, in
Person, John F. Kennedy on the other,
Also in black and white, as it were, and was.
Weird what they can do with video
These days—it's more than movie "magic."
Soon, the whole movie's
Taking on tragic dimensions—not
The story or anything, which can
Only be dismissed as pure American lunacy—
But the very fact that the picture
Was deemed worthwhile to make in the first
Place. Sometimes, it's true, I begin

To think that God is, must be, a
Conservative Republican who only
Admires and approves of unrewarding work,
Penultimate thrift, and impossible moral
Rectitude, if not merit. Tricky Dick's
Mother, we are now being shown, was
Into psychological child abuse; the kid
Playing the young, dismally black-
And-white Nixon-as-a-boy looks,
In truth, a great deal more like Nixon
Than Anthony Hopkins does—I
Guess they couldn't wait around for
Him to grow up. Joan Allen as Pat
Nixon is the only adult who looks any-
Thing like her namesake, and the
Film is going to her, for all that, thank Thespis.

Young, sibilant gay boys out in the hall
Are visiting "Justin," a real prick of
A multi-earringed neighbor-cum-gay
Boy across the way. The noise! Like
A cage full of hissing snakes! How to
Be fair in reporting this? Time to fly,
Myself, though, because we know
How this story ends. Uh-oh. Here comes
The lead-booted, drum-and-bugle-corps music
That indicates that the "Kennedy-assassination-
Plot-idea"—that is to Oliver Stone what honey is to
Bees, as gambling was to Dostoyevsky—
Is now boldly, circumspectly entering the
Scene. Tricky Dick seems to have
Been up to his old tricks in this one,

Too—he knows, in some toothily inchoate
Manner, that what went on wasn't just
Grist for the political historian's mill.
And why not? I, too, during some
Of my choicer psychotic moments,
Have sworn I was part of that plot,
And taken the fall, and known the
Friday-afternoon sting. Now, military drums, more
Creepy music, and eerie talk of
Castro, the only one among the
Many in this film who isn't
An unavailing ghost. Also, Pat
Nixon smoked cigarettes, heavily.
Or are they—like all of this strangely bizarre,
More-traumatized-than-traumatizing movie—
An historical prop, of which I deeply—
Puffing away—approve? Time to walk
Out on it all. The movie's getting
Too dark, and I don't mean from
Underexposure. Oh, to go,
And never come back, like them!
Or, to be able to guess at what
We once thought we believed.

A CRITIC'S HUNCH

Every man has his price,
But yours is so incredibly low,
My illness can only afford to let you go,
My hunch, my unusual inner stillness.

As my faith in my fellow man
More than falls apart
I will rip you out of my heart
And my affections,
Seeking more solar directions.

I end as I finish:
With a full plate of spinach.
You're gone for good,
And all of those who agree with you,

Who agreed upon this fee with you,
The price I won't let you pay.
I cannot "make amends" up
To those whom I no longer know,
None of whom were friends
In the first place. God, I wish I could
Say this to you in person,
To ultimately heighten and worsen
Your position, which is one of coercion,

Entirely. But it might put a stop to you
Responding with your usual bland remarks.
As a tip to you, I say the blind
And only the congenitally blind
Can see in any kind of dark.
For that, I will not be scorned.

All my cherubim come horned.
In fact, everything now
Is to my utter delight:
The furtive fleeting-of-the-light
At the return of a November day,
An early-January afternoon
Of some near-future winter having its way.

I know how wronged you feel:
It is because you are wrong,
You and the pack of thieves and self-disowning faggots
You've chosen as your extended family.
Family? They are simply maggots.

Fortunately, I am the only poet
In the immediate family.
I am also, by your word, the fallen woman,
The pariah. But what pariah is not the new messiah?

I get up when I please
And seldom fall to my knees
Anymore, angry, rebellious, critical, a renegade.
Worst of all, I still find solace
In my always-welcoming loneliness,
My undeniable verbal prowess, and my dislikes,
Which are my own, impregnable palace.

Two Boys

1.

Well, David, you came and went
In rapid succession. "I like to get to know people
Better," you explained, feet up. Then,
A little later, after nothing had happened:
"Well, Gerrit, I'll put my number
Right here next to Michael's."
And you left, after gazing at me first.

I admire you for your moral
Courage. I'd like to wake up
Around three this morning, hearing your
Theme song, like Norman Maine does
After first meeting Esther Blodgett in
A Star Is Born, knowing, "He's
The one! Gotta find him!"

But I'll probably just wake up
Hungry. David was here, now he's gone,
Probably for good. So goes
Another night in the city, summer,
1979. Goodbye, David. Good night. And thanks
For the good advice about not smoking anymore.

2.

If I get to sleep tonight,
It will be an American success story.
Damn, Dan, why did you have to leave that message on my
    machine?
To cancel Thursday night, *pas de doute.*

It's as hot as a vulva in this apartment.
I started to take a taxi home from this boy's house,
Then stopped and got out. "The youngest member of the
      First
Fuckers of America," he had beamed. I went back to the bar

And cruised you, and you, wondering about it.
Blonde, lithe, with an Adidas box full of phone numbers.
Shoots coke, he said, because snorting it is no high.
What kind of person is this? Rick, twenty-two.

There was nobody else around at the bar; everybody had left.
So did we, and later, alone in the cab on my way home, a
      poem came.
But that phone message blew it. Damn it, Dan!
Oh Rick! Oh torrid night. An American success story.

THE LIGHT OF THE WORLD

If somebody asked me
Who my main influences
Had been . . . but who
Would want to know
A hard thing like that?
I ran around to three galleries
Today. I couldn't find hot cross
Buns in any of four groceries.
Tonight I walked out on
Easter Vigil at St. Ignatius.
Broadway this weekend eve
Was alive! Not just with creatures
Of the night, like me, but lilies
Languishing in their stalls,
Loud children's cries, dogs leashed

Senselessly to parking meters,
Yuppies, winos, bums. I missed Mass,
And the Eucharist. But I got
The *Times* early. Why do
Such pomp and ceremony
Have to crowd out
So simple, so great a memory?
It's too late now.
Time to write a nice
Important poem, and this,
Guys, is it. Easter gladness.

Sunday Night, Easter

Again, nothing really phenomenal has happened.
No overgrown boulder has rolled
From the entranceway to a dank, mossy cave,
Unless you transubstantiationally consider
This ace enacted in perpetuum every Easter morning.
Still, we heard nothing at all, we felt nothing.
The rest of the day was gray and monotonous.

I stayed deeply and, as always, dubiously submerged
In one of those twelve-hour sleeps I routinely go in for,
After which I seldom feel rested, although I should.
John returned from St. Michael's about one-ish—
Pretended to be asleep, then sat up and shed the ruse—
Complaining of the fact St. Michael's has foregone
The more traditional mass settings in favor of
The sacral lispings of some contemporary composer-in-
    residence,
Who can apparently out-Duruflé Duruflé.
Episcopalians are like that, sometimes:
You can't speak the word "God" in their presence.
They forget that a human art spurns homespun religious
    chorales
In favor of an ongoing, exclusive requiem to life,
With its unforgettable highs and terrible lows,
Its apprehensive yearnings and trumpet-call for love,
That religion can only approximate in vaporous form.
One major form of religion, for instance, is severe
    depression.
Today, it can be cleanly and clinically treated.

My first reaction upon awakening this morning was guilt
About not having gone to Easter Vigil at 10:30 the night
    before,
At the redoubtable St. Joan the Martyr's over on West End
    Avenue.
Then I suddenly remembered—it hasn't proven
So redoubtable of late, what with AIDS-scandal rector's-
    boyfriend's
Death, and a perennially quarrelsome vestry out of the
    Jetsons.
And my presence there, or not,
Really only had something meaningful to do
With the handsome brass-and-velvet collection plates
Passed from aisle to hand and back again, like a handshake.
I think we must do those good works unto ourselves, first.

Jesus had not, no, had never insisted upon a church,
Or, at the most, he suggested a very private one,
And that's where I spent the balance of my day,
Hunched over my typewriter, head bowed not in prayer, but
    trance.
Some inspiration informed the piece I was working on;
More did not, and I struggled on, as with Christ's sufferings.
Still, wasn't this just a sketch to get the structure seen,
No matter how temporarily, garishly skeletal,
Cornices missing, moldings, even columns—no, not a
    column,
Not deep down—to be added later, when it groaned and stood
On its own, signifying what it would stand for, and how.

Tonight, work put aside, I think each blessed Easter Sunday
Should be a day of not-easy self-resurrection.
Jesus didn't do it for us; we must demonstrate what we've
    learned.
Lacking his apparently God-given transphysical powers,
We must nevertheless each endeavor to eke out
(A shaman's cry just leapt from the street to my window)
The necessary renascence of the everyday, each day including
    Christmas.
Nothing calamitous happened, and nothing transporting—
How long will the hoary tale bear telling?
We were just glad to be there, over succulent cranberry juice,
At the end of an edgy and endless afternoon,
London broil with red bliss potatoes for dinner,
And serious, unspoken doubts about the existence of an anti-
    Christ,
At least, not on such a quiet, rainy night.

THE EASTER STORY

Easter is an animally lonely day,
Whatever the date or its spring weather.
Christ has risen and been put away.
Now we can all forget Christ together.

A couple who claim to be invincible friends
Invite a mutual friend to Easter dinner, excluding you.
They have different concerns than Easter, other ends.
You do alone the loathsome nothing-to-do.

How celebrate the rite of rising
When your heart's exploring subterranean depths?
How can it come as at all surprising
When every day we rise from simpler deaths?

Now it's time for you to take your stand.
All you can do is wait in all the sun for nighttime,
Body prone on bed, hand on unwavering hand.
Easter has never come at the right time.

JIMMY YAWNED

Those who experiment with me
Prove much merriment to me.

How goes the simple sonnet?
"A living pox upon it,"

And a huge red rose,
As time's trellis will disclose.

But betray betrayal!
Hammer not in the bloody nail!

Feast with me, and be my wife!
Come, kiss me Kate, and be my life!

Something else passes between them,
Though no one has surely seen them.

"The sleep of reason breeds monsters."
"And," yawned Larry, "bad punsters."

But really, aren't nightmares scary
Even though they're imaginary?

Now Hepburn and Tracy, they were swell,
As was Koko the Inkblot from his inky well.

What more walls must I shimmy or hills climb
To find a wooer more divine?

Damn. There you go again with the religion,
Making everybody else your pigeon.

A pair of cocktails set by the sea,
On a glass table, inviting mystery.

No one is behind it, no one before.
Skip the end and tell me more.

Club soda does not remove most stains
Any more than the woods stay dry when it rains.

Agghh! It's that tooth again,
Pain becoming divine truth again.

PARTY

We spent the balance
of the evening discussing
the Hemlock Society. After
Fran and Goofy left,
Mollie fixed Jim
with an ice-congealing stare.

Matisse follows his
bliss. He goes
straight through to
the ending, of strange bliss,
in a dark Tribeca sidestreet—
inside-out aesthetic carnage,
or so Beverly demurs.

To think, Dinah
Shore in my home!
The original inextinguishable
nuzzler, smuggler, chimp-faced Dinah!
Nothin' could be finah!

Something's deathly wrong
with this country, says Rosemary:
Prozac is sweeping the nation.
Ted and his "friend"
take the opportunity
to stride in inopportunely.
I look up from
your eyes for a moment
and find reality vacant.

Toxic

Remember when the clock ran backwards?
When the void was at a standstill?
I fret and I wring my hands, still,
At the days of that night. I lack words

To describe the joy and the horror,
When the river ran red and stinking.
I sit here alone, coolly thinking
Of the joy that preceded the terror,

And the voice at my side that kept whispering,
« *Tu es enchaîné, donce misérable.* »
« *Ce génie est trés venerable,* »
The voice would mutter, lisping,

As the earth spewed forth its contents,
And the city streets rocked and trembled,
While the swallows dipped and dissembled,
And love became utter nonsense.

A Sudden Summer

I.
Yes, there was a period during which
Everything went smash. I didn't do
Much about it—what can a mouse
On a glue trap?—but I was duly amazed
And distracted. You saw. I knew.

It was as if the concerted forces
Of silly evil had conspired only to laugh
At me, personally, ontologically, however
Much possible and legal. I gulped pills.
I took cabs from under the seat.

I read out the wrong people
Constantly, as if this were a plain necessary,
If strident, part of the plan.
I had to go on living, or it was curtains
For me, and I don't mean red velvet.

How had Job gotten through? He had exculpatory
Friends. I had a "support system,"
None of the members of which
Were particularly good friends—
Just gamely supportive. It was not my favorite time.

Still, spring and I can go a few rounds
Playfully, even with all that.
But summer—summer has me instantly
On the mat. I can't think in
Desultory heat, I can't concentrate,

I can't make love, and you must to
Make it through it all. Summer makes me
All iron and self-will. Insults were heaped
Upon injuries, sweat ran like lifeblood. I was
Alone, which I usually like. This was different.

2.
Autumn, heaven bless it. Daytimes
In the sixties, nights plumbing the high
Fifties, and I now have confidence
They're coming back, and I'll learn how
To sleep all over again, which is infinite trust.

What had happened? A dangerous rite
Of passage, to the point of mandatory
Courage, much lying around, a certain necessary
Disregard for the claims of all others,
A direct way out, a symphony of personal

Jubilations—no, that's now.
That's the new meteorology, the
New, clear me, as unexpected a wrap-up to Hell
As the original catastrophe had been unearned.
I'll always remember the lemonade you served

One night during the crisis, allotted
Sparingly, because I said I only
Wanted to "taste it," hah, hah.
Much, much more, was desired,
And your hand was steady as it poured.

OPHELIA

Whenever, like Ophelia, I'm in jeopardy,
I dream I am she—in time's aspic
(the eternal river)—an eternal fish
locked beyond words. The moon
beams down on me, has the face
of Hamlet, his dark body invisible,
but is not he, has not even read the play,
and lifts me warm and fresh
into a second life where I dance
with him in a field of flowers
whose names
I cannot remember.

ON THE WARD

Since getting friends in was a matter
Of doctor-review-board, a lot of the patients
Never bothered to take off their robes
And pajamas from the first day anyway.
Dinner the night I was there
Was spaghetti and creamed spinach.
The receiver end of the ward phones stank,
As one nurse put it, and she went forward
To daub the mouthpiece with alcohol swabs.
One boy moaned most of the time,
A whiney, adolescent wail that made no sense
In terms of content. If this was
The "dual diagnosis" unit,
I'd hate to have seen the psycho ward.

I went because of family pressure
And the feeling I needed a vacation from drugs,
Including alcohol. I was soon disabused
Of the notion that any vacation was in order,
At least, on these premises.
Psychiatrists probed, hammered, chiseled
The delicate psyche as it wept.
Mental prongs were applied to the cranium.
I have never seen anything like it,
So woebegone and without hint of hope or healing.
I plan to do an expose on mental wards now,
Called "Crazier Than Before."

I put up such a fight that night
In the form of hysterical, teary breakdown,
I think they were going to be glad
To see me go. I knew I would,

And fell asleep on the doper Klonopin
With a Jehovahlike assurance
I would be out of there tomorrow.
Call it a spiritual experience, if you will.

I was out the next day, that silver tomorrow.
I neglected to say the floor had only two showers,
Sadly not in use, while strange Hispanics
Bent like Degas dancers with towels in the halls.
I told them I would take care of the detox
At home. They frowned, they railed, they warned
What life outside could do to you.
I wanted so much to get back outside.
But I knew they were on my side.
By characterology or looks, I didn't belong there.
That would have been obvious to a herd of cows.
Call it what you like,
But when I bungled my way into a cab
And had my first cigarette in twenty-four hours,
I went to Dionysus' heaven, suddenly all body.
I came home to vodka and lemonade.
You see, I am an addict of Ibsenesque endurance.
I had no business being there in the first place.
Then Moses parted the Red Sea.

THE ANSWERING ANGEL

Oh! That grief should be so real,
And so sincere, so deadly in earnest,
As to exclude any other passion
But for the fiery furnace.

So keen, so sad, so absolute,
With the added intensity of fear,
The hopelessness of middle night,
Excluding any other dignity.

I grimace in a prayer, then rise from my knees,
And burn the candle high and wide,
A cameo of him inside.
Nothing else could possibly matter,

But what mattered in relation to him,
The late-parted, dear-hearted in his sin.
Oh! That grief should be so real,
And doesn't mind how we might feel.

In a Blackish Mood

I don't really know
What ill-meaning friends
Would have me do,
Except see them
Through my crises,
The only things
I've ever willingly
Owned, but
For my grief.
Maybe now, with
Ancient Indian summer
On the way, something
Banefully positive
Will happen, like
Your becoming a new
Mouseketeer—the

Eternally dying Annette,
Like it or not? What fits
Well is not always meant to,
No matter what the size—
Freedom, in other words,
Defers to custom. People now

Come in two varieties: the evil,
And the relatively less
Evil (but only rela-
Tively). Something hurt,
Where nothing could.

My life is the laboratory
For other people's
Experiments, I've always
Held.

Did you get conveniently
Past the unwholesome rush
Of your story when you
Got to the part about
Addiction foreseen and
Foresworn, down to the
Open-ended symbolism you
Threw in for cheap grins,
To make it stick? No. Instead,
You told the fable of your
Few convictions, hiding it

All behind Dame Conviction
Hisself. But that was timely,
In the Age of the Happy
Victim and all. As ever, I
Feel this weird excitement—
Tantamount to a brief
Attack of heartfelt mania—
As I approach the end,
The printing, and the dissemi-
Nation-for-one of this poem,
If that's what you call it.

Something or other must
Lie ahead. The waning lilac sunset
Goes perfectly with the October
Air-conditioning—there will
Be no midnight recanting this time,
Not this time or soon again.
I still love you—it's not
An option. And people who
Come on as anything but
The real center of the
Universe are the
Purist solipsists.
Savvy?

DEAD AGAIN

for Audrey Ushenko

Value life? They're mostly afraid of death.
It probably falls short of crystal meth.

To walk into a room comprising strangers
Poses, for a human, certain basic dangers.

I'm no good at life, so I've survived.
They're the living dead, and they shouldn't have been revived.
They promise certain healing in vast conformity,
Looking on any given license as deformity,

And recommending "eternal vigilance" as a motto.
I've only been able to maintain it when I was blotto.

We all die, and all of us sin,
And it's vanity for some to think they win.

I don't have the heart for it much longer,
When ignoring my heart is supposed to make me stronger.
Boredom, of course, is the mother of invention,
But this is boring beyond any creative intention.

These people simply aren't what I admire.
A lot of smoke with them doesn't mean fire.

I'd like to go away, and maybe not come back.
Can I arrange for a massive heart attack?

I'm no longer young, and I was never slim,
And I think God wants me to come have lunch with him.

A place like this fabricates tomorrows.
Your joys are offal, and your sorrow, sorrows.

I had a hope that I also had to quash.
I'm beginning to look like ripe summer squash.

But I keep coming back, and keep getting the stare.
They can't help it—I'm not all there.

I'm hearing voices, but nothing too odd.
They're the Devil, Mother, and Father, the Trinitarian God.

I still enjoy myself when admiring male beauty,
It's my sustenance in life, my rhapsodic duty,

Although I myself am no longer attractive,
Except for my eyes, hazel and active.

You might call me an intransigent romantic,
But, come on, boys, let's not be pedantic.

This is a vigorous rubdown with an iron glove.
Some die off. Others fall in love,

And dredge up their pasts in telling detail.
They forget, the future sells retail.

How many times have we heard this story?
Ensconcing the worst so as to bury the glory!

The spirit is harder than the letter of their laws.
Heads nod approvingly to big applause.

Talking with any one of them is exploring outer space.
Running with cripples, who can keep pace?

Punishment comes in the form of liberation.
If this were a radio show, I'd flip the station.

I'm somewhat hopped up from it, and a little forlorn.
I got used to death the day I was born,

But this never forgiving yourself, sinned against and sinning—
You're always at the bottom of some numberless inning.

Don't they know that adult evolution
Proceeds along the line of mature revolution?

Too much unholy fervor,
And you lose yourself, all your mortal nervure.

I wear things out, then I wear them.
If people frighten me, I double-dare them.

What would you do if you were I?
I'm only as bad as I have to be to get by,

To be good and dumb, feckless as a fox.
No longer left alone, I quake in my socks,

Because no one here appreciates economy-sized agility,
This type's only humbled by the thought of their own
    humility,
And half are half-dead, the other half, retired.
I'm feeling so much better, I'd die to be inspired.

PETRUCHIO

Once again, my fate
Is saved by fate,
My life snatched from disaster
By arriving a little too late

Once more, a timely pratfall
Lands me on my toes
And my infernal patience
Secures me a position, and a rose

Once again, my wicked life
Takes the wrong turn
On the right day
And sunshine is what I earn

Once more, into the breach!
And I'm still breathing
While others who have all the luck
Sit there, seething

One more time I elude
God, with timely praying
Only for myself. For this,
He talks me into staying

Once again, my fortunes
Reverse, this time not for the sour,
Just in time for me to make
A lifetime, singing, of an hour

Once more I tell you
Happiness is just a thing
You dream of. True
Joy finds you on the wing

Once again, so bold and bald
As to light where no land remains
In the middle of the ocean,
With a chance to use your brain.

RESUME

It's the inevitable being-left-alone,
The not-knowing, the no-longer caring,
And the gift that is given back to need,
The lack of essential daring.

It's the daily putting of getting-to-sleep
Above all and anything else,
And the dreams that cramp, and the needless waking,
To "Good morning," said to yourself.

It's the delaying tactic that never works,
Until its not-working spells delay,
The putting-off of paying the piper
When there's nothing left to pay.

It's the daily giving of too-much-credit,
Where credit is not due.
It's the light-of-your-life gone out for good,
A loss that will see you through.

There's the painful wanting and too-hasty getting,
And the not-having-anything-left,
And passion that's something-worse-than-passion,
The heart most alive when bereft.

There's the waiting-and-waiting in hurrying-around,
For someone to call your name,
When it shouldn't, and won't, leave any mark.
It's no different, all the same.

To Keats

I take a mid-sized yellow tab, and soon
I'm on a cruiser heading toward the moon.
I take the pill because I am in pain,
And always was, and will be soon, again.

I lie down on the blue sheets of my bed.
Half-awake, half-dreaming I was dead,
Excited by the thought, yet brought quite low
By something I will never need, or know.

Wake up at noon? And then what will I do?
There are so many things I could pursue.
Adoring them all, I want it understood:
The good we do is not just done for good,
But for all time, all perpetuity.
Doves would cry, you wrote so easily.

THE DEEP END

for John Ashbery

Something drastic and wonderful is about to happen.
We hover around the midnight pitch like angels*
Who've heard one "Gloria" too many,
We have humanly learned that learning is hard
For the ever-dying, and shared, and expensive.

We each have our little secrets,
Which we wear outdoors like perfume or cologne
Across the wide Bavarian plains,
And the steaming heaps of sheep leavings,
The whimsical memory of doll dishes, from a child's
        viewpoint,
The slag, the mercy, and the victor's head.
Stars reflect and deflect off our remarkable sense of things,
Our likable, daily awakenings
Which are more valuable than sleep,
And less barbaric and sudden. Yes, that too.

And so we learn to take it seriously,
Maybe even stay on another night,
Leading to another semi-successful daytime,
Reevaluating, if necessary, the timely descent
Of One who will, no matter what they say,
Come back home again. Our petit point is done,
Just the beginning of many Sunday exercises
In clearing the conscience, making way
For the March of the Wooden Soldier
From out of Lesbos' workshop.

Oh life! I expected more of you,
At the very least the banshee wail of a good castrato,
Or a sweetheart's kiss to her returning sailor.
But there are no wars anymore.

There is nothing left to shout about either,
Because we watch it all from underwater
Of a redeeming rain that almost overtook the sky.
There, now—you've stepped in a proper puddle.

But there are no more diamonds either, hon.
It's like life in a Gloria Grahame movie—
And she never was a star in the sense of Donna Reed.
But she was cheap and lovely and gentle,
And we do well to assay to memorize
The concept, refurbished for us by zealous walkers:
Dance, and you sleep with the piper;
The picking and talking that can rend a person apart;
That it is not tears that graze the cheek, but acid,
As the lights grow dimmer from our first love on.

CODE Y

At forty-six years of age
Going on 2001, I start to
Admit: there is "a great deal
Of fun to it all," as some old
Wiseacre once observed, if sex,
The greatest fun of all,
Is still best left to the
Young New Conceptualists.
The quote is from A. A. guru
Bill Wilson—I couldn't
Help it, so help me. Speaking of
Which, someone from A. A.—
An organization I rarely support
With our tax dollars—described
Me recently, on a strange 10:00
Occasion at his place—as "oversexed."
Hmm. What he wanted to do to me
Was tie me up to the bed
And leave me there until he got
Home the next morning. I insistently
Refused, and if that is oversexed,
Well, I must be seventy-six going on
One-hundred-minus-naught,
And soon, forever.

To get through a gastronomically
Difficult lunch in a coffee shop
Recently, I told myself, reflecting
That my S & M A. A.'s age was fifty,
"Don't trust anyone at all
Over five." In fact, I concluded, don't
Trust anyone who's already born.

Haven't we been through this already,
And isn't it the last word
In ono-aesthetic boredom?
Since I am invincibly "oversexed"—
Love-starved is the way I read that—
I lustily long for my old wheezing Europe,
My kingly right of resignation, and a
Stately, mid-life renunciation
Of all the running around, whining about
The rain, like Mercury Himself on a bender,
The idiot getting and spending speeding one along,
The life spent hiding one's fabulous light
Under any convenient bushel, "Any old sport
In a dorm," as a poet friend once described
His brilliant career and life to me.
Blissfully unborn, dutifully unwanted,
I spend my days taking long bubble-baths
In essence of twelve-step-forbidden "self-pity"
(There go Tchaikovsky's symphonies,
Michelangelo's slaves, and Judy Garland's acting),
Age 2001 heading toward Mars and Venus,
Toward a new constellation I'm taking up
Quarters in, making headquarters of.
"Close Encounters of the Seventy-Eighth Kind"
Has been my personal apocrypha,
Which has never been a joke to me
Or to anyone who loves me. Advanced age brings
Advancing possibilities, over the curried water,
Toward the only target—and it's not the "self."
At my death, I will rest easier if I never henceforward
Hear the words "judgmental," "spiritual," or "dysfunctional"
Again. Everyone's dysfunctional, poets must be judgmental,

And spiritual usually means "out to lunch for now."
It was never meant to be an "easy birth," thank you
Edward Albee, in his paean to the unprintable, *Virginia Woolf.*
On the stage of Carnegie Hall, "I know . . . I know . . . "
I suspect she did, or something like it.
When atom bombs of love go off,
Somehow we must know.

ON THE SUBJECT OF TEEN SUICIDE

They're too beautiful to live,
Really, which is all the more
Reason they should. As fully

Underdeveloped as they are,
They come clad in shining garments,
Which they then neglect to shed, all

Mock witness and lack of conscience,
None of overly specious heart, like ours.
They have divested themselves of any need

For further longing. We ancients stop;
We tear our dwindling hair, and look around us,
Further amazed to find that they're not there
Anymore, to find that death has found us.

I LOVED YOU ONCE IN SILENCE

I loved you once in silence.
But silence, I found, can do violence.
So I said everything I had to say.

You said you loved me, too,
But had other roads to pursue,
Plans to make, people to see.
Your amorous itinerary did not include me.

No, by Jesus, I'm not mad.
It's just that I've got it bad.
Silence is not always golden,
Although you're in no way beholden.

Funny thing—I can say it,
And by word, you will not betray it.
By act—well, there hangs a tale
We're not going to finish.

Wipe your mouth when you eat spinach.
Wear rubbers in rainy weather,
And beware the day, oh, beware it, dear,
We love in silence together.

LAMENT FOR MATTHEW SHEPARD

What to do?
O, what to do?
Where to go
If not to you?

      Where to go,
      And whom to love?
      How imagine
      God above?

      Why go on,
      O, why go on?
      When you've already
      Come and gone?

When to meet again,
How to say?
When to mourn is to honor,
And to hate is to pray.

Last Things

Never, never be too honest—
That way, the blame doesn't fall.
There is no high, kid,
Like the unmitigated low,
No success that doesn't follow
A first, succoring failure, first.

But it's too late in the October evening
To worry about your chances at anything,
Too early in a newly unfolding midnight
To have much earnest, if adoring, traffic
With dim-witted, skirt-chasing Fortune.
There was a time, in the ever-changing long ago,
When only the darkest liturgical music
Got you through the night, if that.
But since you finally converted—
To what? your friends all wonder—
Only Charpentier will do—
All that military folderol—
Along with that prototypical bad Catholic,
Amadeus Mozart. I loved the move,
Often more than the music itself.

I'm not going anywhere without me—
"Don't share, and you'll soon share alike,"
As even my Gemini Twins must agree.
You compose a little, you drift off to sleep,
You come up for air, you try to squint,
You get there by your art, which is to make do.
See you in the funny papers, kid,
Where life is a rut and a piebald riot,
Your virtue, at last, concealed in total fun.

SOMETHING BRIGHT AND BEAUTIFUL

for Darragh Park

I think man should be exonerated.
What's a summer without boys,
Or a swoon without the arms to fall in?
Perhaps purely man's penis should be exonerated,
But where does that leave us girls?

Without a pot to piss in, as they say in Setauket.
I put my bags in my traditional room.
Freshened up, changed clothes, and look!
There's a generous smattering of stars above the tree,
The great, spreading elm, once dormant and wise.

It is taking every last ounce of my strength
To write this, enfeebled as I am
By spiritual gout, fatigue, and lack of love.
But! There was love in your preparation tonight, Darragh P.,
Right down to the shortbread compound in wrap,

Sweet as a mother's lap when you were too little.
Having gone this far, we turn back gladly
To the shingled palace where the lurcher resides,
And bedtime comes too soon, however long it takes,
And no song is forced, or sung beyond its moment.

To Have These Few Things

To have these few things:
The ability to do a few things;
The intelligence to comprehend
What may not be an expected end;

Sunlight in the caves of winter;
A friend to remove the lion's splinter;
The queer force of soul to be forgiving;
Makeshift arrangements for triumphant living;

To have these few things:
To stop short when a bird sings,
To know which of your loved ones are,
To note the pith and pliancy of a star;

To have these few things is to have many,
In a life as mint as a new copper penny.
The rest of it is anyone's guess.
Having these few things, and nothing less.

JESUS

Touch me on the forehead
With your kiss.
I have never been
As excited as this.

I remember our walk
In deep sand.
Without saying much,
You took my hand,

Took hold. Oh, friend,
I have never been so excited
As this: the chance of all
Injustice being righted.

Even the sun
Kowtows to your name,
And the waves lap up
On the sand, like your fame.

How could a plain saint
Be so human?
You enter any human chamber
There is sufficient room in.

Beauty pales.
Dearth rears up and dies.
At night, I hear you
Hear my cries.

Touch me on the forehead
With your kiss,
Even this,
I will abandon this!

CREDO DIABOLIQUE

My heart is with the pagan.
My heart is with his lust.
I also have known desire
That wasn't dust-to-dust.

My heart is with the thief who hung
Beside Jesus on the cross.
Could a sure promise of Paradise
Make up for this uncanny loss?

My heart is with the hunter
Who never eyes his prey,
For fear he'd grow too fond of him
And starve another day.

My heart is with the terminal case,
Whose incredulous soul first dies,
Before a willing body follows suit,
And the room is filled with flies.

My heart is with the suicide,
The evil one who's lame,
The rank transgressor, the pederast,
My heart is just the same.

THE LUZHIN DEFENSE

I've turned a corner today,
Through too much fuss and strain,
And now I don't know at all
What country I'm standing in.
The doctor says there is no

New countryside to be a part of,
And so, *mon cher* Valentine, why worry?
But I worry to the game—
This game to which my doctor
Says I'm addicted—I don't
Think I understand. I like the dancing
With my fiancée; I bathe regularly
And take long walks around the grounds.
It's only one's own finger

That can hurt one, turned back
And shaking and pointed inward. God,
If only autumn would commence soon,
And you—you wouldn't see me for the skies.

PRELUDE

I think we're all
As innocent as the day
We were wrackingly conceived,
Not in the jostling and bruising and bites,
But in the curtained sunlight,
In the thickening eyes.

The Persistence of Memory
for John Wells

You are not my reason
For living, but you present one
Strong argument for it.
Often, you make a good case
Just by being there,
For bearing with these daily
Ecstasies of unchecked misery—
Which you, sometimes, can add to,
Immeasurably, on occasion,
But never the you I know.

You definitely aren't a lover,
Nor I am one of yours, but after
Twenty-some-odd-and-uneven
Years of physical and metaphysical
Personal engagement, of beseeching
Altercations and rueful beatings-up,
Of ritually voiced woes,
And voiced, alas, again—our funny
Polyphony of pain with giggles,
Sobs rolling on the floor—
After two decades of being a kind of
Telepathic husband and wife,
Older and younger brother, each,
I wouldn't give up
For James Dean revivified—or,
It would take much agonized thought.

There's even something tonic in the way
We share our desperations now,
Unable to much alter or alleviate

Them either way. Such sharing
Is a brief, mutual exaltation
Of our mutual culpability
For deeds done and undone,
Or fresh-faced guilt, our gifts,
Or very real and sustaining life gifts,
Which can also make for a lot of fun.
There are, too, the things that both repel
Each other's souls and make
Them strangely, uniquely complementary,
And even make certain others discreetly
Obsessed with our less-than-sanguine affairs.

You are no longer a night
On the town, nor I the ultimate credit-
Card flasher—they've flashed
Right out of sight—but pepper-
Charred hamburgers and Val Lewton
Movies on my sixth VCR in as many years.
You can live on a little money,
I think, lying on the bed,
Thinking in script like this,
Three A.M., again, it is,
Watching you sleep on your back,
On the funky futon, like the stone effigy
Of a saint inscribed on the lid
Of a big marble coffin, up one of the
Infinite corridors of St. John the Divine,
A cathedral I remember your not liking.
I just want to thank you for your slumberous
Presence. But your facial demeanor
Is so relaxed and noble—almost
Light-emitting—I think, maybe you are

Being thanked, honored, anyway,
In a dream more fit to dream.

I'm in early-A.M. mental agony, as always,
About everything I've ever thought
Or acted upon or regretted regretting,
Everything I've said, dreamt, or loutishly
Imagined: such as my relentless daytime
Braggadocio that alternates
By the minute, softly as the changing
Of a shepherd's watch, with self-despair
That would turn away demons. I want
To wake you up—aren't there twenty
Years of understanding here?—and ask for
Your help, but I don't know for what.
And I want you to get your sleep; you have
A 10 A.M. dentist appointment
For which you must rise at 8 A.M.
To take your prophylactic antibiotics.
On the other hand, I don't want to flip out
Completely, noiselessly, with a scream, unattended.

It isn't that you're mean,
But then you don't know what to say.
You're still one of the reasons
I won't try suicide again soon—
You'd be so angry and offended, again—
And I think, beyond that,
Just that much more lost in the life
You once said you never asked for,
Than I, even enduring the pit and the rack,
Can imagine myself capable of bearing.

100

Evesham Station, 9/9/74

I am standing on the platform.
I haven't traveled on a train
since I was a child.
I've forgotten what you do
with the luggage.
I am holding a brown leather briefcase
with my name embossed
in gold letters on it.
My sister gave it to me this morning.
She cried when I went.
She is sixteen.

I check my watch with the station clock.
"Is it right?" I ask a man
in a brown suit
who looks used to this kind of thing.
"Of course! It has to be!" he says.

I comb my hair—
it is perfect,
it is sleek—
I am new and sleek.
"Where are you off to?" a lady asks.
"Ruislip in Surrey," I say.
"That's a long way," she says.

Five minutes.
People are all around me.
They are used to this.
I check my ticket.
It is in my top pocket—
the top pocket of my jacket
which fits me perfectly.

The train is coming.
It is loud, so loud.
I have tears in my eyes.
No one is seeing me off—
we thought, best not.

I wait for some of the others
to get in. You put the luggage
on the rack above the seat.
A paper. I ought to have bought
a paper.

I am sitting in the train.
I can see my face in the window.
I am on my way to Ruislip,
nothing can stop me now,
and I am perfect—
no one can fault me.
I am going down to Ruislip
and I am perfect.

Two Poems Beginning with the Same Line

I.

I feel that my work is finished.
Every poem is my last,
In no sense diminished
By its happening so fast.

I feel that each work is an ending,
Which starts and winds up here.
That the message I am sending
Is a final one: dear.

2.

I feel that my work is finished,
That I may at any moment die,
Without any of it being diminished.
It makes me want to cry,

Because everything is done now.
Now you may look.
I am a poet who has written how.
You write the book.

St. Stephen Looking Heavenward

for Tom Carey

Is there anyplace left to go?
Anything more to do?
You are perfect, and you know
I always am, with you.

If a star is left in the sky,
Or there's a place to go when we're free,
We'll arrive on the breath of a sigh,
In the tawny arms of the sea.

"Who are those people I saw?"
"The Devil, and Her wife."
"What a loathsome maw,
Good reason to end all life."

No, not just yet. There's a way
To go on when Eternity's gone:
Love will have the last say,
When Love is said and done.

APPENDIX

INTRODUCTION TO GERRIT HENRY'S
THE LECTURER'S ARIA (1989)
by David Lehman

Gerrit Henry was a sophomore and I a junior at Columbia College when we met in the fall of 1968. Kenneth Koch, whose writing course I had taken a year earlier, invited me to sit in on a class with his new group—he knew that I, as an editor of *Columbia Review,* was eager to recruit good writers for the magazine. It was the week of Kenneth's sestina assignment, and the cleverest example was turned in by Gerrit Henry. "Sestina" was one of the six recurring end-words in his poem; a "Mrs. Sestina" made an appearance, and the poem referred to itself jubilantly as a "sestina sestina." An even better Gerrit Henry poem, "The Young Poets," was published in *Columbia Review* a little later. It remains the most marvelously accurate send-up of what it was like to be a young poet in that intensely literary Columbia community:

> There was a kind of introspective silence for a moment,
> Then a new and male young poet timidly entered the room.
> "Will you read my poem?" he asked, and gladly they agreed.
> The young poet Alan answered first, "This poem is fine,
> Except for one thing in this poem I do not like."
> He looked around the room and the others agreed,
> "The one thing in this poem we do not like
> Is the use of the word 'beer.'
> Otherwise this is a long and good poem,
> One of ours," he looked about him in the room
> As the others began to nod sleepily,
> "You will be welcomed here."

In the twenty years that have passed, Gerrit Henry has quietly accumulated an impressive body of work with a stamp all its own—what critics used to call "a distinctive voice" back in the bad old days of the good young poets. Only a portion of that work can be represented in this chapbook, which is bound to whet the appetite for more. Ezra Pound declared that poetry had better be at least as well-written as prose. Gerrit has revised the spirit of that injunction: he wants poetry to be as lively and as buoyant as a lyric penned by Dorothy Fields for a Jerome Kern melody that Billie Holiday might deliver with Teddy Wilson at the piano and Lester Young on tenor sax. And he wants to find a poetic language capable of communicating the glamour and the romance of Fred Astaire singing "Night and Day" in *The Gay Divorcée*. There is therefore something unusually operatic about the poems in these pages. A mused-upon forties photograph of "Judy Garland and Frank"—Sinatra, as the title needn't specify—becomes a kind of musical comedy icon. At times Henry's lines create an effect a little like what you'd obtain if you could persuade the diners in a coffee shop to break into spontaneous song: "Who cooks oats? Bundles you up in coats?" ("Cathedral"). My own favorite is "At Thirty-Eight," where the poet returns to the scene of the rhyme—the songwriter's rhyme, that is. Here is Henry's heartbreak hotel, saved from sentimentality by the irony implicit in exaggeration:

My days of crying over love are over.
Although you couldn't really say I'm rolling in clover,
My heart is swept bare as the White Cliffs of Dover.
My days of crying out for love are over.

The Lecturer's Aria is, in the words of the title poem, "strictly gorgeous."

About the Author

Photograph by Neil Grayson

GERRIT HENRY (1950–2003) is the author of three books of poetry: *The Lecturer's Aria* (Groundwater Press, 1989), *The Mirrored Clubs of Hell* (Little, Brown and Company, 1991), and *Couplets and Ballades* (Dolphin Press, 1998). He was a contributing editor for *Art News* and wrote regularly for *Art in America*.